Festival Decorations

Anne Civardi & Penny King

Crabtree Publishing Company

Craft Workshop

Crabtree Publishing Company

350 Fifth Avenue	360 York Road, R.R.4	73 Lime Walk
Suite 3308	Niagara-on-the-Lake	Headington, Oxford
New York, NY 10118	Ontario L0S 1J0	England OX3 7AD

Edited by **Virginia Mainprize**
Designed by **Edward Kinsey**
Illustrated by **Lindy Norton**
Photography by **Steve Shott**

Children's work by
Emily Ashworth, Emma Carrington-Brook, Amber Civardi, Charlotte Downham,
Lucy Figgis, James Jarman, Emma Loraine-Smith, Alice Masson-Taylor,
India Masson-Taylor, Georgina Mew, Victoria Moss, Archie Parrack,
Susie Roberts, Georgina Smith, Jessie Stratton, Florence Turner

Created by

Thumbprint Books

Cataloging -in-Publication Data

Civardi, Anne, 1948-
Festival decorations / Anne Civardi & Penny King
p. cm. – (Craft Workshop)
Includes index.
Summary: Discusses various occasions celebrated around the world - the new year, spring,
harvests, Christmas, and death - and provides instructions for related crafts.
ISBN 0-86505-790-7 (pbk). – ISBN 0-86505-780-X (rhb)
1. Holiday decorations – Juvenile literature. 2. Handicraft-
– Juvenile literature.[1. Festivals. 2. Holiday decorations.3. Handicraft.]
I. King, Penny. 1963 - . II. Title. III. Series.
TT900.H6C59 1998   745.594'1--dc21   97-32136

CIP
AC

First published in 1998 by
A & C Black (Publishers) Ltd.
35 Bedford Row, London WC1R 4JH

Printed in Hong Kong by Wing King Tong Co Ltd

Cover photograph: This Tree of Life comes from Mexico. Every year in November, on the Day of the Dead,
Mexicans place these candlesticks on family graves and light the candles to keep the spirits of the dead happy.

Contents

4   World festivals

6   Tools and tricks

8   New Year

10   Happy New Year

12   Spring

14   Step into spring

16   Harvest time

18   Happy harvest

20   Christmas

22   Christmas decorations

24   Family festivals

26   Family fun

28   Life and death

30   Special times

32   Index

World festivals

Since ancient days, people all over the world have celebrated important times. At these festivals, people remember events from the past or the special days of their religion. They celebrate the arrival of the new year, the end of a long, cold winter, harvest time, birth, marriage or death.

At almost every time of the year, people all over the world have something to celebrate.

Festivals tell us a lot about the history, way of life, religion and beliefs of the people who celebrate them.

In spring, at the Hindu festival of Holi, people run through the streets and throw buckets of colored water over each other.

People decorate their homes, have huge feasts, set off fireworks and fly colorful flags. They dance and sing. They wear costumes and masks and have large parades.

Buddhist monks in Tibet perform a special dance to bring in the new year. They wear masks to drive away evil spirits.

Guardian Deity Mask, Tibet The Horniman Museum London

This book tells you about some of the festivals celebrated by people around the world.

You can learn about the Chinese tradition of bringing in spring with bright windmills.

You will discover why Japanese families fly colorful fish banners outside their homes on Boy's Day.

You can also find out about a unique contest held every Christmas in Krakow, Poland, to build the best nativity scene. You will read about the Hindu Festival of Lights, known as *Diwali*.

You will learn how to make decorations to celebrate these festivals. Look at the pictures in this book of decorations made by other children. Use their ideas to make exciting decorations of your own.

Tools and tricks

To make the decorations in this book, you'll need to collect bits and pieces, such as old shoe and cereal boxes, cardboard rolls, scraps of cloth, wool, raffia, shiny candy wrappers, sequins, ribbon, popsicle sticks and cork.

You may also need to buy a few things from a craft or hobby store.

Paints

Ready-mixed poster paints can be used for these projects, but you might try acrylic paints. They cost a little more, but are brighter and shinier. You will also need fabric paints to color cloth.

Fabrics

Felt is the easiest fabric to work with because it does not fray, comes in bright colors and can be bought in small amounts. If you don't feel like sewing, you can glue felt pieces together.

Scissors

You can use pinking shears, which are scissors with zig-zag edges, to stop fabrics from fraying.

Glue

For many projects, you will need fabric glue or white craft glue. For bread dough, you will need wood glue.

Stuffing

Cotton wool is perfect for stuffing dolls and other shapes. You can also use newspaper or scraps of cloth.

Making papier mâché

Put some flour and white craft glue into a mixing bowl. Stir in enough water to make a paste, about as thick as creamy yogurt.

Tear sheets of newspaper into small pieces. Brush a thick layer of flour paste over the shape you are covering, such as a balloon or orange. Cover it with a layer of newspaper. Brush on more paste. Repeat until there are four layers of newspaper. Finish off with a layer of paste and let it dry.

Sewing

The simplest stitch is a running stitch. Thread a needle and knot the end of the thread. Pin two pieces of fabric together. Push the needle through both pieces and, at about ½ inch (1cm) from the edge, pull it out again. Make another stitch a little distance from the first one. Repeat this. When you have finished, make four or five stitches on top of one another to stop your sewing from coming undone.

Hemming

Turn over about ¾ inch (2 cm) of fabric and sew a running stitch close to the edge.

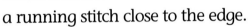

Cutting fabric shapes

To cut two pieces of fabric the same shape, first draw a pattern on a piece of paper and cut it out.

Fold some fabric in half and pin the paper pattern onto it, making sure you pin through both layers. Carefully cut around the edge of the pattern, through both layers of fabric.

Making bread dough

Cut the crusts off six pieces of sliced white bread. Crumble the bread with your fingers. Put the crumbs into a mixing bowl. Add wood glue and 2 tablespoons (30 ml) of baby powder. With your hands, knead the mixture into a thick dough. Put your bread dough decorations into the freezer to harden.

Making eye holes in a mask

Put the mask up to your face. Ask a friend to draw circles on it, where your eyes are. Ask an adult to cut out the eye holes with sharp scissors.

Working with clay

Use self-hardening clay and roll it in your hands until it is soft. If you want to add extra pieces onto a model, use a knife to scratch the two pieces you want to join, as shown below. Wet both pieces with water and firmly press them together.

Smooth the clay with your fingers, so the join doesn't show.

New Year

People all over the world celebrate New Year with parties, dancing and music. It is a time to plan for the coming year and to think about the future.

Hindus in India and all over the world mark the start of the new year in October or November with a Festival of Lights, known as *Diwali*. People clean their home and welcome visitors and friends inside.

They place little clay lamps, called *divas*, in their windows and outside the door. This is to honor Lakshmi, the goddess of wealth. Hindus hope she will visit their home and bring them good luck in the coming year.

The Chinese new year falls between late January and the middle of February. At this time, Chinese children are given little red and gold packets containing money known as 'lucky money.'

Children may also be given dolls, dressed in red and gold, and holding money packets in their hands. The Chinese believe that red and gold are lucky colors.

In Japan, people hang fans around their doors to bring them good luck in the coming year.

For centuries, both Japanese men and women have used fans. There are two kinds. The ones that fold are called *uchiwas*. Those that do not are called *sensus*.

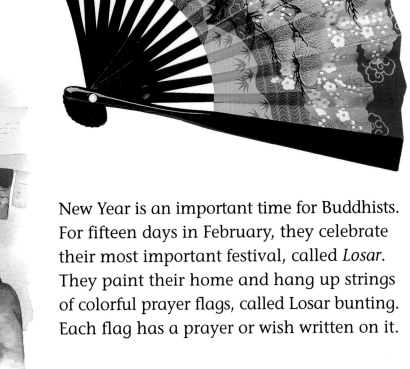

New Year is an important time for Buddhists. For fifteen days in February, they celebrate their most important festival, called *Losar*. They paint their home and hang up strings of colorful prayer flags, called Losar bunting. Each flag has a prayer or wish written on it.

Happy New Year

Welcome in the new year with these bright and cheerful festival decorations.

Little lamps

Shape some self-hardening clay into an elephant and a small bowl. (See page 7 for instructions on working with clay.) Let them dry. Use poster paints and a gold felt-tipped pen to decorate them with patterns. Put a candle in each lamp and ask an adult to help you light it.

Lucky money packets and dolls

Fold a rectangle of colored paper in half and glue two sides together to make an envelope. Draw patterns onto it with a gold felt-tipped pen.

From red felt, cut out two dolls of exactly the same shape. (See page 7.) On one, glue a felt face, a small purse, shoes, hair, hands and a belt. Use a running stitch to mark eyes, a nose, a mouth and the arms. Put the two shapes together and sew around the edges, leaving a small gap. Stuff the doll with cotton wool and sew the gap.

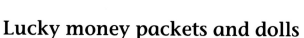

Bright bunting

Cut out lots of rectangles from pieces of fabric. Turn over about ¾ inch (2 cm) of a short end of each rectangle and hem it. (See page 7 for instructions.) Tie a long piece of string to a big safety pin and thread it through each flag. Hang up the flags in your room.

Fabulous fans

With felt-tipped pens, draw a Japanese-looking tree and patterns on a piece of white paper.

Leave the background white or color it with a felt-tipped pen. Fold the fan into pleats. Glue or staple together the base of the fan. Paint a popsicle stick black and tape it to the back of the fan.

Spring

In many parts of the world, spring is the time to celebrate the end of the cold, dark days of winter. Flowers and leaves begin to grow and animals have their young. Spring is an exciting season when people celebrate new life.

Fabergé egg The Royal Collection © Her Majesty the Queen of England

Eggs have been a sign of new life for many centuries. This beautiful egg was made by the famous Russian jeweller, Carl Fabergé. He created it for the Tsar of Russia in 1914 to give to his wife, the Tsarina, at Easter.

The egg is made from gold, platinum, and green, pink and white enamel. It is decorated with hundreds of precious diamonds, emeralds and rubies. Hidden inside is a picture of the Tsarina's five children.

Each spring, Christians around the world celebrate Easter. On the Saturday before Easter, people in Poland decorate real or wooden eggs. They are covered with delicate and beautiful patterns.

On Easter Sunday morning, Polish people decorate their breakfast table with these eggs. They add green branches, pussy willows and animals made from candy or an almond and sugar paste.

The Yaqui Indians of southern Arizona celebrate Christian Easter stories with dances. Some of the dancers wear painted masks made of paper or animal skins. They carry wooden swords or daggers. Other dancers wear headdresses decorated with paper flowers and ribbons. They shake rattles made from dried gourds. Once the celebrations are over, the Yaqui burn the masks and weapons in a big fire.

At the Ch'ing-ming festival in Hong Kong, children welcome spring with shiny paper windmills. The windmills whirl around as they catch the wind.

This is the time when families remember their dead relatives. They visit tombs and weed and tidy up graves. Red paper money is burned as an offering to the dead.

Step into spring

Create an egg fit for a queen or paint eggs to decorate your breakfast table on Easter day. Make your own noisy rattles and shiny windmills to welcome the spring.

Jewelled egg

Cover a small blown-up balloon with papier mâché. (See page 6 for instructions for making papier mâché.) When the papier mâché is hard, paint the egg a bright color. Glue on sparkling decorations, such as sequins, glass beads, ribbon and foil paper.

Pretty painted eggs

Ask an adult to help you hard-boil some eggs. When the eggs are cool, paint them with poster or acrylic paints. When they are dry, paint on colorful patterns.

Noisy rattles

Cover an orange with plastic wrap. Layer on papier mâché. (See page 6.) When the papier mâché is hard, ask an adult to cut around the middle and take out the orange. Cut a hole in the bottom, big enough for a round stick to fit inside. Join the halves of the rattle with two more layers of papier mâché.

Put dried peas, beans or small pasta into the hole. Push in the stick handle and use more papier mâché to set it in place. When it is dry, paint the rattle and decorate it with patterns. Glue ribbon around the handle.

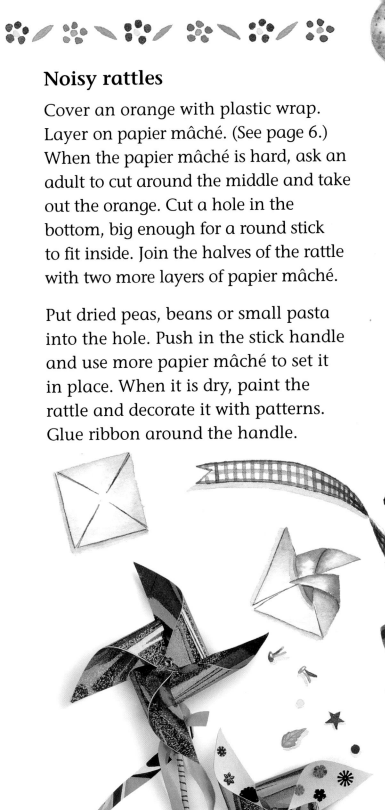

Whirling windmills

Cut a square of colored foil paper. Draw two diagonal lines across the back. Cut along the lines, stopping about ½ inch (1 cm) before they cross. Pull a pointed end from each triangle towards the center. Push a pin through all four ends and through the center of the square. Push the pin through a piece of a plastic straw ½ inch (1 cm) long and into the end of a long stick. Decorate the stick with paint and ribbons.

Harvest time

Fall is the time of year when people give thanks for a good harvest and for the rain and sun that helped their crops grow.

Dogon mask © Edward Parker

The Dogon people from Mali, in West Africa, celebrate harvest with masked dances. Some of the masks look like trees. Others look like animals such as antelopes, buffalo or lizards.

This dancer is wearing a lizard mask that is over 3 feet (1 m) high. During the dance, the dancer bends from the waist and scuffs the ground with the lizard's head to raise clouds of dust.

At harvest festivals in Britain, churches are decorated with flowers, fruit and vegetables. Sometimes, a loaf of bread, made in the shape of a bunch of wheat, is placed in the middle of the display. After a service of thanksgiving, the food is given to needy or sick people.

Each year, the people of Kerala, in southern India, celebrate a harvest festival called *Onam*. Children pick flowers to weave into colorful patterns, called *pukalam*, which they give their parents. In return, the children are given new clothes.

Corn dolls, made from the stalks and ears of corn, are still part of many harvest festivals. People believe that the dolls will bring good luck and plenty of crops in the next year. This doll, made of oats, silk, lace and ribbon, comes from Montenegro in the Balkans.

Corn Dolly The Horniman Museum London

Happy harvest

Celebrate the end of harvest time by making your own animal mask, tissue-paper flower mat or corn doll.

Wild lizard mask

Paint a scary face on the bottom of a shoe box. Ask an adult to cut out a space for your neck and holes for your eyes. (See page 7 for instructions.) Cut out the shape of a lizard from cardboard. Paint it and tape it, as shown right, onto the top of the shoe box. Thread and tie a rubber band, long enough to go around your head, through a hole in each side of the box.

Glue pieces of wool, fabric or raffia to the top of the mask for wild hair. You could also glue on shells and feathers.

Fabulous flower mat

Cut out a round mat from loose-weave fabric. For the fringe, cut short pieces of raffia or wool and thread them, one by one, around the edge of the mat, ½ inch (1 cm) from the edge. Knot each one. For flowers, cut large tissue-paper circles of one color and smaller ones of another color.

Glue the middle of each of the small circles onto the middle of each large one. Lightly pinch the middles together. Glue the flowers in circles all over the mat with one big flower in the middle.

Corn doll

For the body, make a thick bundle of dried grass or raffia. Tie string tightly around the neck. Pull two small bunches of grass for the arms and tie a ribbon bow around each wrist. Decorate the doll's body with lace, scraps of cloth, bows and foil. Use glass beads for the eyes.

Christmas

Christmas is a time for friends and family. People get together to share delicious meals, sing carols and give gifts.

This nativity scene, showing the birth of Jesus, is known as a *szopka*. It comes from Krakow in Poland and is a copy of St. Mary's church in that city. It is made from shiny paper and cardboard.

Each December, a contest is held to see who can make the most beautiful *szopka*. Some are over 9 feet (3m) high. The winners get a prize, and their szopkas are shown at the museum.

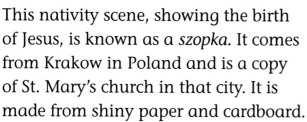

In Sweden, the Festival of St. Lucia marks the beginning of the Christmas season. Girls dress in white and wear a wreath of leaves on their head. They carry a candle in honor of Lucia, the Christian saint of light. The girl who is chosen as the Lucia queen leads a procession from house to house, wearing a crown of candles on her head.

This Christmas angel was made in the United States by the Shaker people. For over two hundred years, the Shakers have lived quietly in small farming communities. They are famous for beautifully made furniture and crafts.

In Ecuador, women make these bread dough figures, called *figuras de masapan,* as colorful Christmas decorations. This art can be traced back to the small bread dolls that were made to celebrate All Souls' Day. These dolls, made in village bakeries, were placed in cemeteries for the hungry spirits of the dead.

21

Christmas decorations

Build your own nativity scene to decorate your house at Christmas. Sew a cloth angel for the top of your Christmas tree and make bread dough decorations to hang from its branches.

Magical nativity scene

Glue together different-sized boxes, such as match boxes and small cereal boxes, to create a church with two spires. Cut a window out of one box. Use felt-tipped pens to draw a picture of the baby Jesus and his parents on white cardboard. Stick the picture inside the window.

Cover all the boxes with colored foil candy wrappers. Use glue and tape to stick all the boxes together.

Glue a foil-covered foam ball on top of each spire. Decorate your nativity scene with flags, a shooting star, a clock and sequins.

Cloth angel

Cut out two angel bodies, of exactly the same shape, from plain fabric. (See page 7 for instructions for cutting fabric shapes.) Sew the two bodies together, leaving a small gap. Stuff the body and sew up the gap.

Lie the angel on folded fabric. Draw a dress shape and cut it out through both layers of fabric. Sew up the sides and sleeves. Put the dress on the angel. Tie ribbon around the wrists, neck and ankles. Glue cloth heart shapes onto the dress. Sew on thread hair and eyes.

Cut out two wing shapes. Sew the wings together and stuff them. Then sew them onto the angel's back.

Bread dough decorations

Flatten balls of bread dough. (See page 7 for instructions for making bread dough.) Cut out stockings, stars and Christmas trees. Smooth the edges with your fingers. Make a hole in the top of each shape. When they are dry, paint them bright colors and hang them with pieces of ribbon.

23

Family festivals

All over the world, there are special days and festivals for members of families. On these days, people give their relatives presents or do special things to show how much they care for one another.

Boy's Day Carp © Eye Ubiquitous

On May 5, a festival is held in Japan especially for boys. Outside their home, parents fly giant paper kites, shaped like fish called carp. Each colorful kite represents a son, with the largest for the oldest boy.

Japanese people think of the carp as the 'king of river fish' because it is strong and can swim upstream. Parents believe that carp have the strength and courage their sons will need in their lives.

24

In India, a festival for brothers and sisters, called *Raksha Bandhan*, takes place in August. *Raksha* means 'protection' and *bandan* means 'to tie.' In a special ceremony, a sister ties a thread bracelet on her brother's wrist to give him good luck. In return, the brother promises to look after his sister.

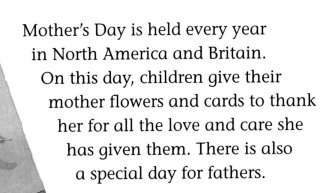

Mother's Day is held every year in North America and Britain. On this day, children give their mother flowers and cards to thank her for all the love and care she has given them. There is also a special day for fathers.

This wool and stone prayer bundle was made by a North American Navaho. It shows a husband and wife and their three children.
The Navaho believe that if they put a prayer bundle in a special place in their home, the Great Spirit will watch over the family.

Family fun

These colorful decorations, with their special meanings, make great gifts for your family and friends.

Dip a small sponge into fabric paint. Press it onto the scales and tail to color them. Print more patches with another color. Let the fish dry.

Place the fish pieces on top of each other, painted sides together. Pin and sew them together, except for the mouth. (See page 7 for instructions for sewing.) Turn ½ inch (1 cm) of fabric over at the fish's mouth and sew a hem. (See page 7 for hemming instructions.) Thread a piece of soft wire through the hem. Shape the wire into a circle and twist the ends together.

Crafty carp

Cut out two fish, exactly the same shape, from a large piece of white cloth. (See page 7 for instructions.) Make each fish's mouth wide open. Place the fish on newspaper and, with a fabric pen, draw on eyes and scales.

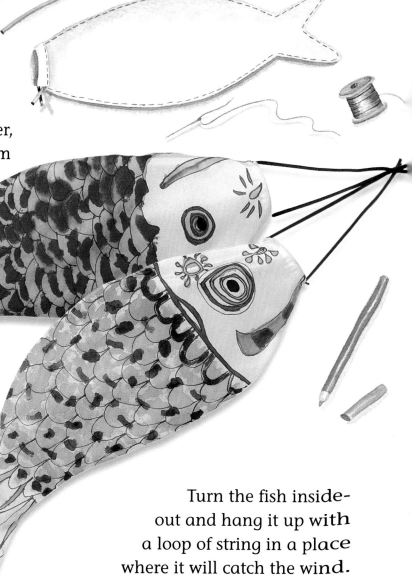

Turn the fish inside-out and hang it up with a loop of string in a place where it will catch the wind.

Every November, on the Day of the Dead, Mexicans remember their dead relatives. They take clay candlesticks in the shape of trees to the cemetery. They are called 'Trees of Life,' and they are decorated with flowers, children, angels and birds.

Mexicans also bring food and flowers to the graves. The candles are lit and the spirits of the dead are invited to join the family feast. Mexicans believe that this keeps the spirits happy.

On the Day of the Dead, Mexicans also decorate their homes. People give each other candy figures in the shape of skulls. They are made of a paste of ground-up almonds, sugar, egg white and lemon.

In Sumatra, Indonesia, beautiful padded decorations, like these, are hung on the beds of new brides and in the rooms where the wedding is celebrated. These decorations are embroidered with gold thread and covered with sparkling sequins, beads and tiny mirrors.

Special times

Build a coffin in the shape of a fish or one of your favorite animals. Create your own magnificent Tree of Life and a sugar skull. You could also make stuffed decorations to give as a wedding gift.

Fantastic lion coffin

To make a lion's body, glue together a shoe box and a smaller box. Glue four cardboard tube legs to the bottom of the shoe box. Stick on cork ears. Paint the lion brown and let it dry. Poke a furry pipe cleaner and wool tail into the box, as shown, and glue it in place. Glue on pieces of wool for the mane and paint on two big eyes.

Sugar skull

Mold ready-made fondant icing, which you can buy in a cake decorating store, into a skull. Shape a jaw and push in eyes. Decorate the skull with cake decorations and candies.